The

Lazy Person's Way to
Wealth

All it takes is doing NOTHING

Law Steeple, MBA
Author of *Tax-FREE Wealth*

IAN Books

An IAN Books paperback

Published by
IAN Books
41 Watchung Plaza, B242
Montclair, NJ 07042

Cover: Gunung Rinjani from Gili Air

Special sales for educational use by nonprofits.
IANBooksEditor@yahoo.com

ISBN-13: 978-1482307139

ISBN-10: 1482307138

Library of Congress Control Number: 2013931919

Contents

Introduction

"The stock market is a device for transferring money from the **impatient to the patient**." Warren Buffett

>Earn 10% to 12% on your mutual funds FREE of income taxes.
>Avoid 1% to 3% fees and commissions on your account.
>Use low-cost mutual funds that are well diversified.
>Use a special IRS account to protect all your interest and gains.

You don't need to do a thing to grow your money in the stock market. That's right. You don't need to gamble on the right stocks or advisor to earn a $500,000 tax FREE! You can do it yourself using the same **low-cost** high-return mutual funds that the wealthy use. **The only thing you need to do is ... NOTHING.**

The wealthy don't sit in front of computer trading all day. They don't waste their money on products brokers sell. Also, now you can grow your money without income taxes or fees. Patience is all you need to become wealthy over time.

People who know their industry know where to invest their money. They know which firms are growing. For instance, investors in Biogen, Qualcomm, EMC, and Kansas City Southern RR saw increases of 6,000% to19,000% in the last 20 years. However, sometimes they make mistakes, like Enron, WorldCom.

Stock traders make mistakes too. Buying and selling is not investing. Most earn 2%--less than inflation! Of course, if you knew anything about genetics, cell phones, internet or rails, you might have put your money in the right businesses. The stocks above tanked for a while but the **lazy person who did nothing** is now wealthy. Their $2,000 might be worth $300,000 now.

Most us do not know which businesses will grow quickly in the future. We have to "settle" for the average returns of 10-12% a year. See page 24. Each of our $2,000 investments would be worth about $20,000 over 20 years in a diversified group of businesses like those in the 10 Vanguard funds some of our clients use.

Most of us know we will never be able to pick the right companies for the future. Wall Street tempts us by claiming they know. Some of us follow their advice and pay dearly. The industry tells us that we need them to get rich. We give up $560 billions year after year. We help them more than ourselves. Trading stocks does NOT benefit us. pbs.org/moyers/journal/09282007/

The wealthy have learned this. They take the business approach to investing and compound their money. We can do the same starting with monthly contributions of just $200. Compounding works only if we leave our money alone. Simple but powerful. Easy, but hard to do. It is difficult to be 'lazy' about our money.

The table below gives us some idea of how fast our money can grow if we invest it in businesses like the ones we patronize every day. We can **do it ourselves and keep more**!

Monthly	Accumulation at 12% per year									
	5	10	15	20	25	30	35	40	45	50
$100	$8,167	$23,004	$49,958	$98,925	$187,884	$349,496	$643,095	$1,176,477	$2,145,469	$3,905,834
$200	$16,334	$46,008	$99,916	$197,850	$375,768	$698,992	$1,286,190	$2,352,954	$4,290,938	$7,811,668
$300	$24,501	$69,012	$149,874	$296,775	$563,652	$1,048,488	$1,929,285	$3,529,431	$6,436,408	$11,717,502
$500	$40,835	$115,020	$249,790	$494,625	$939,420	$1,747,480	$3,215,475	$5,882,385	$10,727,346	$19,529,169

Investing, not speculating, is all about putting our money in actual businesses that are growing so that in the future we can get our money back multiplied many times over.

We play the role of silent partner. We invest in a number of successful businesses so if one fails, we still earn 10-12% a year. We want to pay few fees or tax so that our account compounds at the full 10-12%. We want to invest a fixed amount like $250 a month (about $9 a day) automatically so we can start it and forget it. We want to check our statement only once a year.

I will show you how to set up the **lazy person's way to wealth**. Compounding works best if we do NOT touch our money—NO tax and NO fees. Our earnings are reinvested for the next period. The graph below illustrates what happens to tax-FREE NO-fee compounding over time. We take the $600,000 not $300,000.

Fortunately, low-cost mutual funds and tax-FREE accounts are easily available at no cost. We avoid Wall Street's fees of 1-3% and avoid taxes FOREVER. Following certain simple steps, we can benefit from the FULL miracle of compounding. Many people like you have taken the steps to become wealthy over time in this way. And now the steps have been made easy to execute. **You can do it yourself in an hour**. Complicated steps by the "professonals" slow growth by taking our earnings. Professionals don't know the future.

Tax-FREE v Taxable

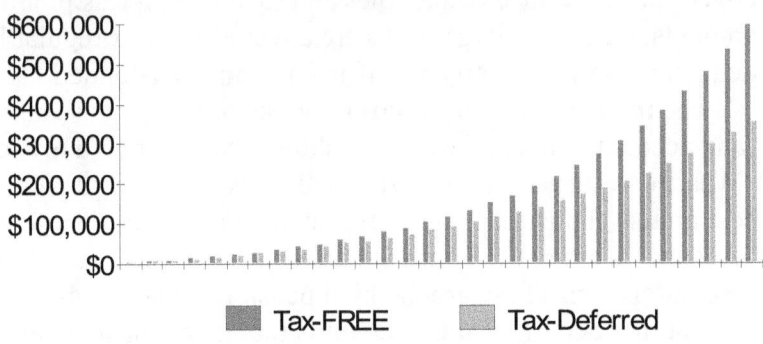

Tax-FREE ■   Tax-Deferred ■

Most working millionaires use **patience** and **time** to build a $1,000,000 fund. They become wealthy by living below their means. They patiently save and invest in their own business or the businesses they own through their mutual funds. They buy shares every month automatically so they can't miss their goals.

I have been in financial services for over 25 years. I noticed that the "lazy" people win. Wealthy people don't trade, don't chase hot stocks or "get-rich-quick" schemes. They usually have their own business and reinvest their profits back in the business. I was most impressed by some school teachers who made under $50,000 a year but had huge portfolios. They didn't know a thing about investing but steadily bought shares in low-cost mutual funds.

The key factor in building wealth is letting our money alone. We have to **maximize the miracle of compounding**. We need to grow our wealth in a tax-FREE account, paying low fees. I will show how to use a special IRS account that can provide a tax-advantaged income source all your life. If you use this account correctly, the **tax-FREE** status is worth over $300,000 extra to you. Taxes are the greatest killer of wealth.

This account, called a "**Wealth Reserve™**" by my colleague, Dan Keppel, grows without taxation as it accumulates. Unlike a regular account, you don't pay taxes every year on the amount your account earned. When you let your balance compound, you can reach your goal in about 30 years. You can do this because you invest in a proven long-term investment—shares of growing companies worldwide—that provides income and growth.

After you accumulate a sizable balance—say $150,000—you

7

can borrow from it to buy things like appliances and cars. You pay cash and avoid paying interest to a bank. You can also use it to cover your insurance deductibles and save paying less premium amounts. Of course larger risks are covered by your regular high-deductible policies. You are self-insured and self-funded.

The **miracle of compounding** works best if you use a mutual fund account at the lowest cost. I show how to set up a low-cost "**Wealth Reserve**™" at no cost. I will show you how to pick low-cost mutual funds for long-term growth and income. These investments are not the ones our salespeople sell because there is no commission. These are the kind pension managers use.

Another benefit of this account is that it can make equal contributions automatic. This is called "dollar cost averaging." It is convenient to invest the same amount monthly. If you and your spouse contribute $250 a month, each of you could have $500,000 over time. By investing a fixed amount each month, you can buy shares at the least cost possible. You buy more shares when the price is low. You buy less when the price is high. You buy at cost.

If your investing is done automatically, you have a better chance of success. **Automatic investing** makes investing a habit. You can't miss making a contribution because you forget about the money coming out of your bank account. The people who succeed at building wealth are those who NEVER stop saving and investing. They use the **lazy person's way**.

You may be thinking this account sounds like your 401k or pension account at work. You are right. Your 401k or 403b works just like a **Wealth Reserve**™ except you *never* have to pay taxes or fees on the accumulations. Most employer-sponsored plans are tax-deferred—you pay later—NOT tax-FREE. The difference can be over $300,000. You will have more to spend when you take the money out. Unlike a pension account, you don't need to take distributions until *you* want to. It is better than an annuity as a legacy for your heirs too. Heirs don't have to pay your taxes.

The **Wealth Reserve**™ may be the best way to provide income later if your employer does not match your deposits. However, you can contribute much more to a 401k than a **Wealth Reserve**™ —up to $17,500 (2013) versus $5,500. Both accounts will compound earnings. One will provide **tax-FREE** income later. The point is that contributions grow without taxes for a number of years. It is best to start with a **Wealth Reserve**™ -- it may provide higher accumulations than a 401k because there are low-fees and NO taxes, zero, $0, taxes, ever.

Unlike other methods of investing for the future, a **Wealth Reserve**℠ can provide a lifetime of tax-FREE growth and income. This is a powerful strategy! It uses the most powerful financial force available—compounding of high earnings over time. It avoids the greatest **killer** of wealth-building—TAXES. You pay no taxes on the accumulations and no taxes on the withdrawals later. And you don't pay broker or advisor fees every year either. You **Keep More of What You Earn** by NOT touching your money!

Below are the 10 steps to create tax-FREE accounts that let you both invest in high-earning securities over time. You must let compounding work its miracle. You pay $150,000 over 28 years for $1,000,000. You don't stop investing when the market goes up or down. You make investing automatic. The miracle happens because you do NOTHING. You have more because you do less!

I will explain the steps to accumulating $1,000,000:

1. Create a $500,000 **tax-FREE** account for each of you.
2. Use a tax-favored lifetime investment account.
3. Compound high earnings over time.
4. Set up automatic monthly contributions for no interruptions.
5. Use low-cost mutual funds earning 10-12%. (See Chapter 3.)
6. Buy groups of stocks of growing companies worldwide.
7. Spend less than you make—live within your means.
8. Buy only the services you need—no "bells and whistles."
9. Manage the account only once a year.
10. Take $80,000 tax-FREE income each year in retirement.

Building wealth requires **patience**. If you are self-employed, you understand that it takes time to build a business. You have to have the right product and then find the customers to serve at a price that enables you to earn a living and a profit to expand.

If you work for others, you don't have to be a genius to become financially independent. Wealthy people control their spending by various methods. Some have goals and budgets that help them build their spending and investing habits. Some are thrifty and don't spend more than they make. Most use CPAs not brokers.

Wealthy people have learned that there is **no quick way** to become wealthy. Accumulating assets requires the investing habit. They learned the habit and saw that the habit paid off over time. Their money compounds and is rarely taxed.

It does not take a lot of time to manage your account. In fact, it takes only an hour to set up a **Wealth Reserve**™ and takes only 1 hour per year to manage it. As master investor Warren Buffett said:

> We continue to make more money when *snoring* than when active.
> berkshirehathaway.com/letters/1996

Building wealth is more about NOT doing something with your investments. Activity in investing usually is the result of fear or greed. Buffett said his holding period is forever—no trading.

People with assets cultivate **patience**. They don't panic when their account goes down. In fact, they buy more assets when others are selling. They know they cannot build a small fortune overnight with a quick buy and sell strategy. Patience allows assets to "grow by themselves." Note on page 22 that the client's account keeps growing even after falling some years. The client never lost money because they did NOT sell in lean years!

People with assets understand that to build wealth they need to keep their money working. They do this by buying only the products they need. In fact, that has become their way of life. For instance, they can afford to buy an expensive new car but they don't because cars lose value quickly. They don't like to lose value. They invest in the businesses they own or in the securities of companies. They improve their future by buying more assets that "grow by themselves." The chart on page 32 illustrates annual stock market growth of $2,000 since 1950.

Wealthy people know about the **miracle of compounding**. Isn't it time you learn? If we invest $250 per spouse, we may have $1 million in about 30 years, $2 million in 39 years. $250 a month is only $9 a day. That $9 a day is building our future life. It provides more security than insurance. In a sense, having assets is the best 'lifestyle' insurance we can have.

It is good to be lazy when it comes to investing for the long term. It is against our intuition, but

doing less . . . gets us more

1

Create $500,000 tax-FREE account for each

Building $1/2 million tax-FREE accounts takes time. If we own a business, it would take a lifetime. We would have to find and sell the right product to the right customer in a profitable manner. It is difficult to come up with a completely new product or way to sell it like Apple has done. If we are lucky, we could buyout our boss after working at a skilled trade for years. Many wealthy people have followed this path.

The Lazy Person's Way to build wealth is to take some of our salary from working for others and buy the stocks of growing companies. We can accumulate $1,000,000 over time, depending on the type of companies we buy. If we use low-cost mutual funds in tax-FREE accounts, it will take about 30 years.

We can understand how this can happen by following the growth of a broad market index mutual fund. **Time is the key** to building wealth for the lazy person. Wealthy people typically invest in many types of investments, businesses and real estate. We begin with investments of $250 a month in funds with many businesses.

If we are going to accumulate $1,000,000 in about 30 years, we need to find investments that can earn 10 to 12% a year, on average, over time. We must understand the reward and risk tradeoff. If we want to have a $1 million in the future, we could wait 80 years for our $500 a month to grow in a bank at 2% or wait about 30 years in a bunch of stocks of companies. We are trading time for the banks guarantee to pay interest **every day**. We don't need that guarantee. We need the high probability that companies will profit and grow over time. That is good for the long-term.

Investing in stocks provides our best chance of success. The value of a stock market index—a bunch of stocks—has varied greatly in any one year. However, over any 10 years, the value has ALWAYS increased. This is the reason wealthy people have most of their money in the stocks of growing companies.

Remember, we are looking for an investment that compounds

our money at 10-12% on average **over time**. The reward and risk profile of owning a bunch of stocks is like owning a business—in any one year, we might have a loss or a gain. But over time we have more profits than losses and thus accumulate $1,000,000.

Range of annual returns of stocks, 1950 – 2000

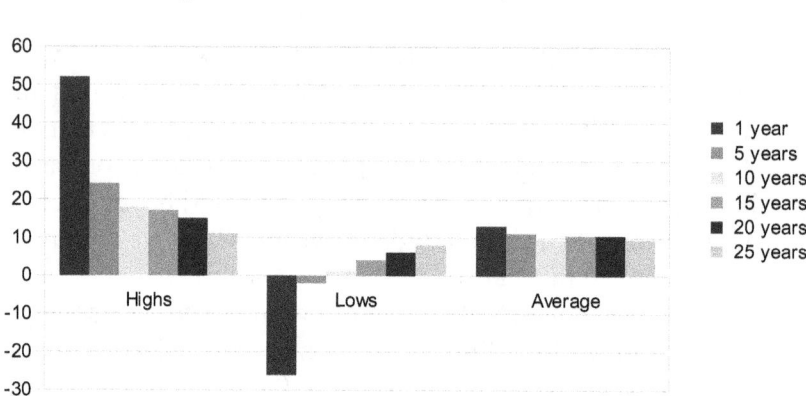

Bank savings are a great place to park our money for a year in case we need it to repair our car, appliances or house. However, bank savings are not really an investment. People who put their money in the bank because they think it is "safe" are not thinking about the long-term. Bank accounts are actually losing money. Inflation is eating away at the value of their savings.

Inflation is historically about 3%. If we earn 3% or less on our money, we are losing purchasing power. This means that it now costs $0.45 to mail a <u>first class letter</u> instead of $0.06 as it did in 1970. Sending a letter went up at about 5% a year. In order to have enough money to mail a letter in retirement, we are going to need to invest our LONG-TERM money in an investment earning more than 5%. This goes for all the money we will need to buy things in the future.

There are few investments that we can buy that have the same long-term annual returns of stocks of growing companies. The graph below presents the relative growth of different types of investments and inflation. Over long-periods of time, government bonds grow at a rate a little above the rate of inflation. Large company stocks like GE and P&G grow at a higher rate and thus accumulate larger values in our account. Smaller companies grow much faster and make our account even larger over time. However, as the graph shows, the index line can be very jagged on a monthly and even yearly basis. Values do go up over time.

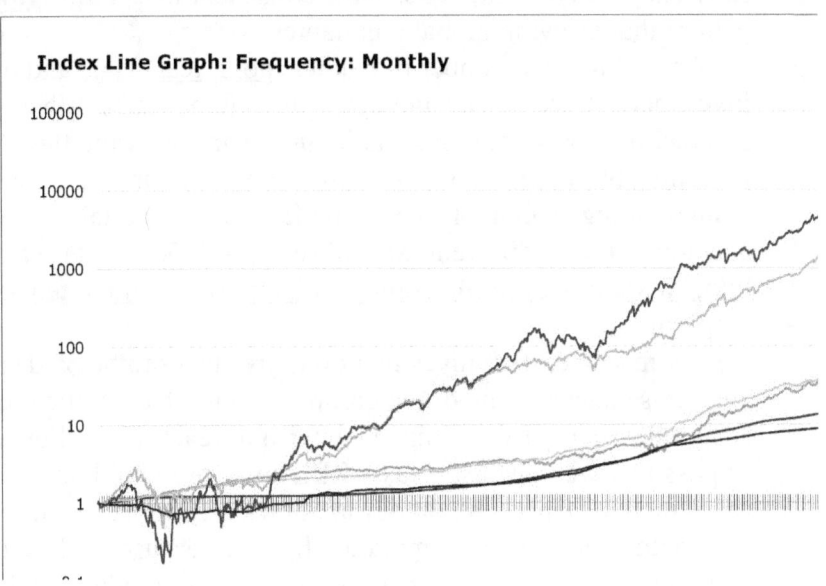

Index Line Graph: Frequency: Monthly

Top line—Small Cap Stocks
2nd line—Large Cap Stocks (S&P 500)
3rd line—US Long-term Corporate Bonds
4th line—Intermediate-term Government Bonds
5th line—US 30 day Government T-bills
6th line—US inflation

Courtesy: Dr. Campbell R. Harvey http://www.duke.edu/~charvey/

This graph makes it pretty clear that in order to accumulate $1,000,000 from monthly contributions, we must buy and hold the securities of growing companies worldwide, at cost, AND pay **zero** tax on the growth to maximize compounding. We can see clearly that investing in growing company stocks is more likely to get us to our goal in our lifetime than investing in government bonds or a bank savings account. Investing requires the long view.

This graph shows the accumulation over time without paying taxes each year on our earnings or annual fees to an advisor or broker. It does show that over most periods greater than 10 years, our account value grows more with stocks.

Some wealthy people also invest in gold, real estate, and

alternative investment schemes. But these investments do NOT usually represent a large portion of their portfolio. These investments do not come without significant costs and significant risk. They do NOT show the same consistent long-term growth pattern that growing global companies do.

According to a number of studies, gold, real estate and other investments have annual average returns under 10%. When we subtract the costs of buying, maintaining and securing these investments, we give up a lot of the gains. We can use an online compounding calculator to become familiar with total accumulations at different rates of return—3, 5, 7, 9, 11, etc. http://www.moneychimp.com/calculator/compound_interest_calculator.htm

For instance, if an investment requires taxes to be paid each year, this cancels some of the compounding effect on the total accumulation over time. Since we wish to reach $1 million as soon as possible, we must use a tax-FREE account to hold our low-cost investments. Depending on our tax bracket (taxable income) we may reduce our total accumulation by half because we lose the compounding effect. The chart below gives us an idea of what can happen in 30 years. Most retirement accounts are tax-DEFERRED not tax-FREE. Taxes have to be paid sometime.

As you have probably guessed, the wealthy have already figured out how to pay less tax on their wealth. The American tax system taxes earned income at higher rates than investment income. Thus we must pay federal and state income taxes, excise taxes, Social Security and Medicare taxes, perhaps unemployment and disability income taxes as well as sales tax on most goods.

For the wealthy, like Warren Buffett, with $ billions of assets, most of his income is from his company stock gains and dividends. He admitted, "I pay at a lower overall tax rate than all of my office employees." He pays only 17% **total** tax. Listen and weep: http://www.youtube.com/watch?v=Cu5B-2LoC4s.

We are not at that stage yet. Most of us have income which is taxed as earned income and goes straight to the government before we have a chance to pay less tax. Even self-employed people must pay taxes as they go—at least once a quarter. Only the wealthy and large companies can afford most tax avoidance schemes. Fortunately, Congress created one for working people. The Roth IRA lets us avoid income tax on the earnings altogether.

Tax-FREE v Taxable

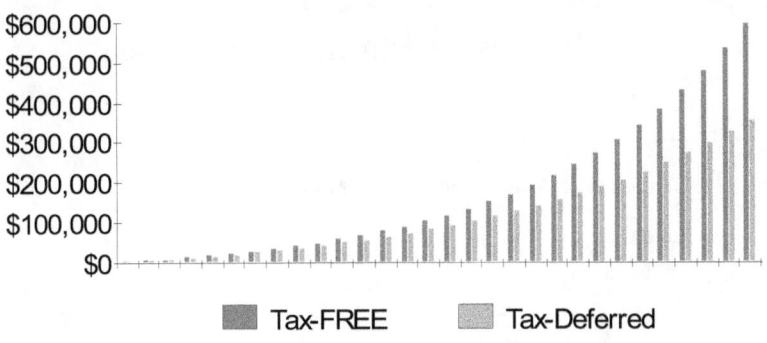

In order for us to become wealthy we must find a way to avoid paying tax on our $1,000,000 accounts as they accumulate. Traditional pensions, 401k and IRAs just delay taxes—taxes must be paid later as the money comes out of the account AND at higher earned income tax rates. Thus even when our investment money is growing it is converted to earned income money for tax purposes. Unlike Mr Buffett, we NEVER get to pay the wealthy people (capital gains) rate of 15%.

Luckily, there is now a solution for us to match the tax advantage that the wealthy. In fact, only we can use it.

Summary: Create a $1,000,000 tax-FREE accumulation.

We use the Roth IRA, a tax-FREE trust, to compound the high returns of the stocks of growing companies over time. We avoid the greatest killer of wealth—taxes—and let time transform our $150,000 in contributions into $1 million. Patience and steady investing make our strategy beat the industry myth of genius stock pickers. This is the *Lazy Person's Way to Wealth.*

Various investment accumulations

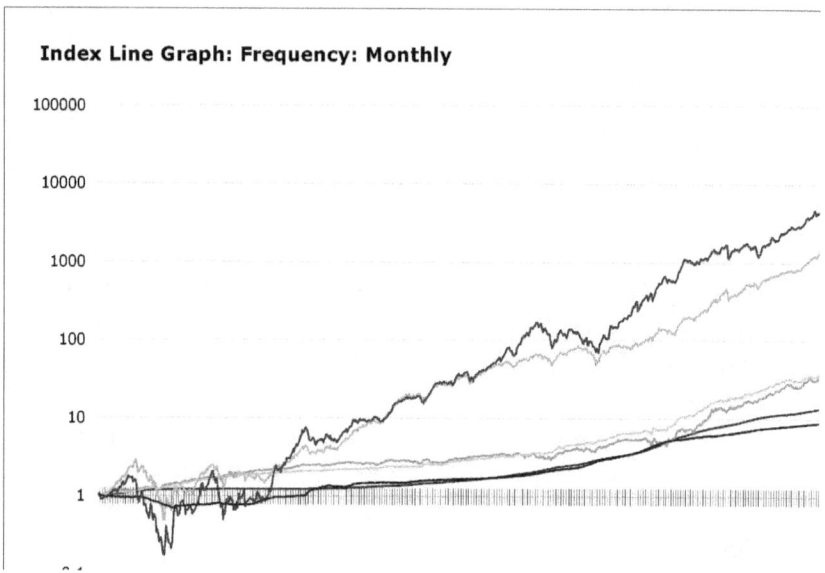

Index Line Graph: Frequency: Monthly

Top line—Small Cap Stocks
2nd line—Large Cap Stocks (S&P 500)
3rd line—US Long-term Corporate Bonds
4th line—Intermediate-term Government Bonds
5th line—US 30 day Government T-bills
6th line—US inflation

Courtesy: Dr. Campbell R. Harvey http://www.duke.edu/~charvey/

2

Use a tax-favored lifetime investment account

The solution to our problem came in 1997. Senator Roth introduced the Roth IRA. This tax-FREE account we call a **Wealth Reserve**™ provides the protection we need to allow our contributions to compound without taxation every year AND later when we take them out, we never have to pay taxes on the earnings, dividends and interest we earn on our money. We don't even pay the tax-advantaged rate of the wealthy!

Ben Franklin was wrong! Only death is certain, not taxes. The only thing we give up with this account is an immediate tax deduction. However, compare the value of paying a little more tax (15%-25% on $3,000) now with paying ZERO tax later. We can spend $40,000 tax-FREE for every $3,000 a year we contributed over time. We can see the fantastic advantage we now have. This is a better deal than most wealthy people have.

Tax-FREE accumulation and tax-FREE income after age 59.5 is a huge bonus. It is like receiving $300,000 FREE on our $1 million account. Also, because we already paid tax on the contributions, we pay no tax when we take this money out for emergencies. This can make a big impact on our borrowing costs when we take money out to buy an appliance, a car, a down payment or living expenses.

Using this account, our total contributions of $150,000 over time grow to over $1,000,000 and we don't have to pay any federal or state income tax on the earnings. WOW! Since we pay no tax, Uncle Sam is really helping us out in meeting our goals. All we have to do is use this special IRS tax haven and keep making contributions. We **Keep More of What We Earn**.

This special account is the IRS §408 trust Dan Keppel named a "**Wealth Reserve**™". We have to follow the rules to gain this amazing tax advantage but the Roth IRA rules are pretty simple—taxed money goes in and tax-FREE earnings come out after age 59

½. We can take our contributions out anytime.

Why is this account special? Every other type of investment account requires that taxes be paid now or later. Mutual funds declare gains each year just like a bank CD and we need to pay tax. Our retirement accounts and annuities are tax-deferred. We pay tax when we take money out. Even life insurance with cash value requires taxes to be paid unless it is a death benefit to heirs. Even assets like individual stocks or ETFs or our own company equity held for long term gains will require taxes eventually when sold. The gains in a **Wealth Reserve**™ are FREE—no tax ever.

Contributions are limited to $5,000 (2012), but may rise in future years. http://www.irs.gov/publications/p590/ch02.html There are income limits of $125,000 (2012) or $183,000 married. We make our deposit to our **Wealth Reserve**™ automatic so we can't forget to do it each month.

We may also invest in our employer's <u>Roth 401k</u> if it is offered. The contributions grow tax FREE forever. We can contribute up to $17,000 (2012). We will have tax-FREE income from the account later. Contributions to a regular 401k can be converted later. We can limit taxes by converting small portions of our 401k (now IRA) each year.

We can make contributions to our Roth 401k only if our employer offers it in the retirement plan. You may prefer to be taxed before your retirement since tax rates are bound to be higher later.

There are no limits on an employee's income in determining if he or she can make designated Roth 401(k) contributions. If we decide to invest $6,000 a year for about 30 years in a low-cost stock fund inside our employer's Roth 401k plan, we could accumulate $1 million with NO income taxation to pay on the earnings. The tax savings might be worth an extra 30% since our federal and state tax payments are avoided. We **Keep More of What We Earn**.

The catch: If we take the *earnings* out before age 59.5, we must pay income tax, unless we use $10,000 for our first home, are disabled, or die. The account must be open at least 5 years to take money out. However, if we take out *contributions*, we pay no tax. If we pay our 'loan' back to our own account, we can still reach our goal. The hard part is leaving our money alone to grow tax-FREE.

Let's say we need $10,000 to buy a luxury used car. As we can see from the chart on page 22, taking $10,000 from an account worth $250,000 is very different from taking $10,000 from one worth only $25,000. Both are contributions and are not taxable but borrowing 40% of the account this early stunts its growth.

Our patient millionaire finds a way to save the $10,000 separately or keep driving the old car. The power of compounding is too valuable to lose by raiding the account too early. One story about billionaire Buffett will illustrate the habits of the wealthy. Mr Buffett is said to have driven (no chauffeur) his VW Beetle long after he became a multimillionaire. Buffett did not like to lose money and a new car loses 40% of its value quickly. He thought that the $40,000 a new car cost, invested at 10%, is worth about $80,000 in 10 years. So he kept driving the old VW.

Monthly	Accumulation at 12% per year									
	5	10	15	20	25	30	35	40	45	50
$100	$8,167	$23,004	$49,958	$98,925	$187,884	$349,496	$643,095	$1,176,477	$2,145,469	$3,905,834
$200	$16,334	$46,008	$99,916	$197,850	$375,768	$698,992	$1,286,190	$2,352,954	$4,290,938	$7,811,668
$300	$24,501	$69,012	$149,874	$296,775	$563,652	$1,048,488	$1,929,285	$3,529,431	$6,436,408	$11,717,502
$500	$40,835	$115,020	$249,790	$494,625	$939,420	$1,747,480	$3,215,475	$5,882,385	$10,727,346	$19,529,169

Most clients are not that thrifty. They use their contributions to buy a used car to avoid new car depreciation and new appliances, vacations, and other necessities AFTER they have a sizable account. When both family wage earners contribute to their Roth IRAs, they can easily reach a quarter of a million dollars in 15 years. That means $90,000 are contributions and then some of it can be used to pay cash instead of buying on credit.

Wealthy people use their wealth to pay cash. They never PAY interest. Paying interest on a debt is the reverse of compounding. Someone else is becoming wealthy from us. The wealthy always EARN interest. They use the chart above or the http://www.moneychimp.com/calculator/compound_interest_calculator.htm to determine what the real cost of buying something on credit will be just like Buffett did. Why give up $80,000 when we can drive the old car a little longer. Buffett could have bought 100 new cars and it wouldn't have changed his wealth or lifestyle, but he didn't. His habit is to live frugally and not look wealthy.

We can use this account (its contributions) to cover our liability insurance deductibles also. We can save thousands of dollars by using the highest deductibles on our car, home and health insurance. Self-insurance is also the way to avoid any changes in our policy costs. Insurers are less likely to drop us if we don't make claims for small amounts. If we take care of our out-of-pocket medical expenses, we may find a low-cost comprehensive policy if we need to buy health coverage.

The rules for the use of our **"Wealth Reserve™"** account are manageable by ourselves. We don't need an advisor. They are found at irs.gov/retirement/article/0,,id=137307,00.html. Our account trustee can answer most questions. We don't need to pay an attorney. All of the large low-cost mutual funds firms are trustees. We will discuss the best firms available below.

We can start this account with any of the firms with no upfront charges. Most do charge an annual fee for the investments and an annual bookkeeping fee. We will consider the specific investment options later. We will use low-cost firms. We will keep more.

It is important to pick a trustee with the least costs since over time the annual costs can really destroy our accumulations. For instance, if we use a brokerage firm as trustee, we might have to pay 2% or more each year on the balance. The difference is huge. If both spouses have a low-cost account with contributions of $250 a month for about 30 years, they could accumulate $1,000,000. If they use a high-cost broker/advisor, both accounts may hit only $500,000. Depending on earnings of 8-10% using a broker/advisor (fees of 2-3% per year), they could really hurt themselves. We need to watch the costs. We will compare firms below.

We can open our account at any age as long as we have *earned* income—stock dividends or interest do not count. Any job will do. We don't even need a job requiring a W-2 to prove it. A part-time, weekend or night job will do. Any cash-only work will also qualify. Accountants recommend that receipts and records be maintained. We could even work for ourselves in a home-office business. This also provides a tax advantage in retirement.

Nontaxable distributions from a Roth IRA won't affect our eligibility for a child's student aid. Later, in retirement, this money won't raise the taxes on our Social Security benefits.

We can make contributions to both our individual Roth IRA and our Roth account at work (401k, 403b, 457b). The limits change each year, so check Pub 590: http://www.irs.gov/pub/irs-pdf/p590.pdf. The 2012 limits are $5,000 ($1,000) and $17,000 ($5,500). (If we are age 50 or older, we can make a catch-up contribution to both.)

Summary: Use a tax-favored lifetime investment account.

Avoiding taxes on our annual gains slipstreams our accumulations. This special account is the IRS §408 trust Dan calls a "**Wealth Reserve**™". We have to follow the rules of a Roth IRA to gain this amazing tax advantage. The rules are pretty simple: pay smaller tax on contributions now in exchange for NO tax on huge gains later— over time, $150,000 is taxed so $850,000 is tax-FREE. We can use the contributions to avoid paying interest to banks for our major purchases. We earn interest, we don't pay interest. The **Wealth Reserve**™ is the perfect tax shelter for working people. And it is free to set up and run each year. In the future, we can spend tax-FREE $40,000 on every $3,000 we invest today. **This is the *Lazy Person's Way to Wealth.***

Actual client account, investing $3,000 per year, 1962-2003

24%	3,720
16%	7,795
12%	12,091
-10%	13,582
24%	20,561
11%	26,153
-8%	26,821
4%	31,013
14%	38,775
19%	49,713
-14%	45,333
-26%	35,766
37%	53,110
24%	69,576
-8%	66,770
6%	73,956
18%	90,809
32%	123,827
-5%	120,486
22%	150,653
21%	185,920
6%	200,255
32%	268,297
19%	322,843
5%	342,135
17%	403,808
32%	536,987
-3%	523,787
31%	690,091
8%	748,538
10%	826,692
2%	846,286
38%	1,172,015
23%	1,445,268
33%	1,926,197
28%	2,469,372
21%	2,991,570
-9%	2,725,059
-12%	2,403,420
-22%	1,874,601
29%	2,412,905

3

Compound high earnings over time

Compounding the earnings is key. The rich get richer—the top 1% take 23.5% of all income (up from 8.9%). And, as many millionaires have said, "the first million is the hardest." If we start with $6,000, it will take us about 20 years of investing $6,000 a year in stock funds to reach $500,000. (And only in a tax-FREE low-fee account.) However, when we reach a **1/2** million dollars, we only have to double our money to reach $1 million. Investors in stock mutual funds, earning 10-12% on average, do this in about 9 years without adding new money. Our low-fee tax-FREE account makes it easier to reach our goal. We pay no advisor costs.

Compounding of high earnings means that we make money on our last period's accumulations. The progression looks like the client's account values on the previous page. Notice that our balance can double in a few good years. This happens because we are not just adding $3,000 per year, but adding up to 38% of the previous year's accumulation to our balance. We are making money on top of our money with no extra effort on our part. During this 40 year period, this client lost money some years. In fact, they lost 14% and then 26% back to back, but then made 37% and 24%.

Wealthy people don't panic. They have learned that compounding over the long term is the only way they can build wealth. There are no successful get-rich-quick schemes. To reach their goal, they know there will be setbacks. No business grows steadily upward all the time. They have seen the losses before and they don't sell their assets in a panic. They remain **patient**.

We will buy assets that "grow by themselves." We will have security because our ***purchasing power*** will grow over time. If we doubt that the wealthy invest in the stock market for security, take a look at the long-term returns for various Vanguard mutual funds where they put their money. These funds have provided investors with $1,000,000 or more for their retirement. During the recent recessions, Vanguard had inflows not outflows.

The wealthy earn 10% to 12% on their money. We could buy all ten Vanguard funds and receive 11.8% total return with less risk than owning just one fund. When one fund is down, others are up.

2012 Total Return	Fund	Long-term Return	Longevity
15.8%	500 Index	10.5%*	since 1976
2.7%	Energy	12.3%	since 1984
18.3%	Extended Market	10.3%	since 1987
15.1%	Health	16.3%	since 1984
20.0%	International Growth	10.8%	since 1981
15.3%	PRIMECAP	12.9%	since 1984
18.0%	Small Cap Index	10.4%	since 1960
10.1%	Wellesley Income	10.2%	since 1970
20.8%	Windsor	11.2%	since 1958
16.7%	Windsor II	10.4%	since 1985
15.3%	Average	11.5%	

*Average Annual Returns as of 12/31/12.

This kind of security comes from our regular contributions ... and patience. The miracle of compounding works its magic on our **Wealth Reserve**™ when we give it TIME. The wealthy give their money time to compound. They don't take it out. They try not to pay tax every year on the gains. They maintain their contribution schedule because each $100 added is worth $10,000 to them later. They use the compound interest calculator so they know the future value: moneychimp.com/calculator/compound_interest_calculator.htm.

Compounding of high earnings requires patience but has a big bang. Most people who become wealthy have to put up with years of waiting. At the beginning of the accumulation, especially if we have a loss or two, we are very tempted to get discouraged and quit making contributions. The account just doesn't seem to adding up to an inspiring total.

It took my client 21 years to get to $150,000. Then it only took 14 years to get to a $1,172,015. After only 4 years, it became $3,000,000. Shortly thereafter he "lost" over a million dollars!

This client stuck with it and was successful in reaching the goal but there are many who did not. Most people who are not wealthy already, have a hard time believing it can happen with their **patience**. They just don't have the experience of how compounding works to keep faith in its outcome eventually.

If you already have a **Wealth Reserve**™ with significant values, you can use it to do your gift and estate planning. You don't have to take the money out beginning at age 70½, unlike the regular IRA or pension. You can let it grow. You can name your family members as beneficiaries which will be effective for both property law and income tax purposes. Obviously, as beneficiary, your grandchild could just liquidate the account and thus lose the value for their "Gift of a Lifetime." Wealthy people use a knowledgable attorney to make sure their wealth passes to those who make the most of it.

Once an account becomes sizable, we don't need to add contributions to it. Usually, by the time we stop regular employment, we aren't making contributions. This account cannot accept contributions unless they are the result of earned income. Some wealthy people continue to work after age 65 because they love what they do and want to continue. Obviously, they don't need to work. The miracle of compounding continues.

One of the best examples of the potential of growth by compounding is seen in the accumulation of investor Anne Scheiber. With below average wages, this woman invested in quality companies which paid dividends and gains. She reinvested her dividends and gains and at her death gave $22 million to Yeshiva University for a scholarship designed to help support deserving women.

Summary: Compound high earnings over time.

Getting "the first half million is the hardest." Since we don't make millions, compounding high earnings is the only way we are going to reach our goal in our lifetime. Compounding works because we leverage TIME and high earnings on high earnings. We *Keep More of What We Earn* with low-fee tax-FREE accounts. Only patience allows our accumulations to compound. This is the *Lazy Person's Way to Wealth.*

The annual returns of growing companies

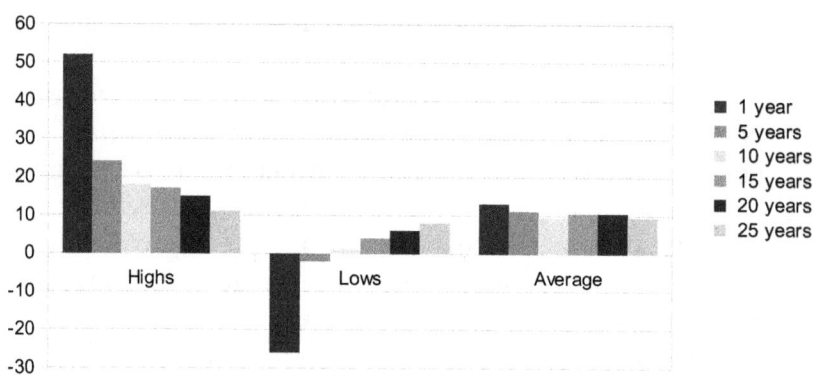

Range of annual returns of stocks, 1950 – 2000

4

Set up automatic monthly contributions for no interruptions

One of the techniques for building wealth is to maintain consistent contributions to our **Wealth Reserve**™. This helps take our emotions out of the process of building wealth. If we do not watch the stock market or our account balance regularly, we will be less likely to panic. If we don't have to write and send the contribution check each month, we won't think about how our account is doing.

Our normal reaction to having money in an account is to watch it, guard it, think about how it is doing, compare its size and rate of growth. We pay advisors to watch too. All of these actions are fine for a savings account. But as a silent partner in growing companies, this is not wise. We have to believe that global businesses will continue to grow. However, most people don't look at their wealth-building in that way. Most people do not think of their accounts as a stake in many growing businesses.

One way we can help change our thinking is to try to put the account out of our immediate concern by making the contributions automatic. Like the Social Security contributions we make every payday, the contributions come out of our pay automatically. This can happen easily with a Roth 401k since our Plan administrator will deduct the amount we specify at Plan enrollment. In the same manner, we can have the Roth IRA trustee debit our checking account automatically every period.

As one client told me, "I never see the deduction, so I never miss it." Of course this client had already identified the $250 he had committed to his $2,000,000 future years ago. He says that he would just waste the $250 anyway. He had been doing that for years because he never took the trouble to set his goals for short-term and long-term timelines. He took my advice and went through his spending on financial services. He used our Guides to find the $250 a month he was wasting on products and services he would never use or need. In Dan Keppel's <u>amazon.com/Insiders-Guides-</u>

<u>Discount-Financial-Services/</u> you will find "tricks of the trade" that we insiders use to buy directly from quality manufacturers.

Many people have trouble keeping up the habit of investing every month. Some emergency always interupts this process. The delay in the periodic contributions causes the compounding effect to be reduced. The interruption is like starting the investment process late. This chart shows us what starting early or not putting off the investments can do. Over time, the delay compounds the lack of accumulation. Starting 5 years later means ending up with HALF the amount we were shooting for. It is hard to believe that missing that $250 a month for 5 years or $15,000 can reduce our total from $600,000 to $300,000. It's easy to say **I will start later**.

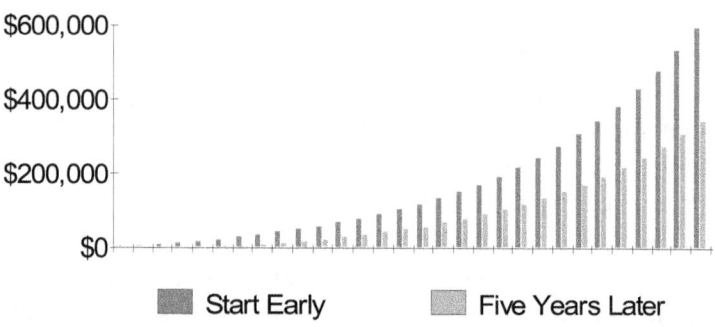

The Value of Starting Early

This is why our contributions to the account should not pass through our hands. We should have the money taken directly from our bank account by the trustee. Contributions are after-tax so you can take them, if necessary, with no tax payable. Nontaxable distributions from a Roth IRA won't affect your eligibility for student aid either. Later, in retirement, this money won't effect your Social Security benefits, which are subject to taxation depending on your income. Even muni bond income is counted in the tax worksheet for Social Security benefits. irs.gov/pub/irs-pdf/p915.pdf

The second reason why this technique for developing wealth works is that when contributions are automatic, we do not have the temptation to try to time the market. Many people want to know the secret to timing the market so that they can invest right at the bottom of market cycles and sell at the peak of the market.

Unfortunately, it is a myth that we can do this correctly. Again, this is our misconception of how building wealth works. Yes there are lucky gamblers. However, they is the exception. We are trying to build wealth over time. We want to end up with $1,000,000 tax-FREE. We are silent partners in building businesses that produce dividends and gains over time. We are NOT placing our contributions on red or black at the cassino.

Our account grows with steady contributions because in the month we buy shares in a mutual fund, we receive less shares when the price is high and more shares when the price is low. Studies have shown that this is better than investing our $3,000/$6,000 all at once. It is not possible to know when the shares we buy will be at their lowest cost in the year going forward. Again, over time, we will own more shares at the least cost because we are buying more when the price is low.

This can be illustrated by considering how hard it is to find the lowest price at any given time in the market. There were ONLY 40 days from 1950 to 2007 that produced 70% of all the S&P 500 index's total returns. That is 40 out of 14,528. We can't possibly know when to buy into the businesses represented in the mutual fund we are using. We will lose money if we become traders who try to time the market well. Traders lose money most of the time. See John Bogle's analysis in _Don't Count on It_, p 169.

The key to building wealth is steady growth. We have seen that over time, stocks of growing companies have the most consistent record of providing 10%-12% annual returns. We just don't know which companies and which time to invest are best. Luckily, we don't have to know. We just need to understand the bigger picture.

The bigger picture is that we want our account accumulation to grow exponentially. We want to take advantage of the miracle of compounding. Since we don't have a million dollars, we are going to have to be patient to acquire it. We want every dollar we invest to count. We have $250/$500 a month to invest so we have to rely on consistent buying of shares to reach our goal.

Accumulations double in value every 8-10 years if they are concentrated in the top two lines. Of course the stock market doesn't move up at 10-12% EACH year. However, our wealth account will double and double and double so that in about 30 years, we could have over $1 million. Notice how the account values in the chart on page 22 for our client double—from $1 million to $2 million in 8 years, even with 3 years of losses. Of course, a million dollars will be worth less in the future because of inflation. But we will certainly appreciate our account values later no matter what our contributions are now. Consistency over time builds wealth.

Cumulative Wealth

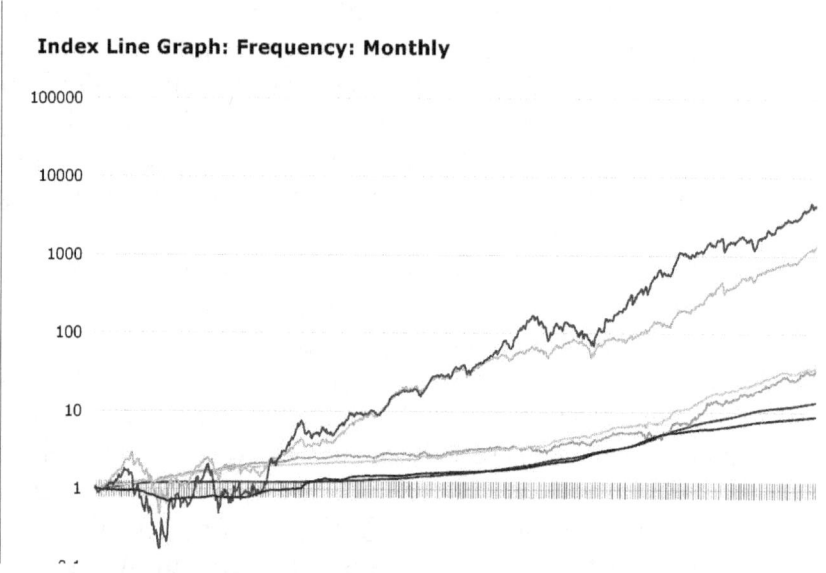

Top line—Small Cap Stocks
2nd line—Large Cap Stocks (S&P 500)
3rd line—US Long-term Corporate Bonds
4th line—Intermediate-term Government Bonds
5th line—US 30 day Government T-bills
6th line—US inflation

Courtesy: Dr. Campbell R. Harvey http://www.duke.edu/~charvey/

And the bonus of this geometric account growth is that it does not quit even after we stop adding our monthly contributions. Once the account has reached a certain mass, let's say after 20 years of contributions or $120,000, it will keep compounding. On page 32 we show you how this worked for contributions of $2,000 to a virtual account invested in the U.S. stock market (top 500 firms) over time.

We can see in the chart "Cumulative Wealth" above that over

time, wealth accumulates at different rates depending on the type of assets we buy. For anyone who invested in smaller companies over any given 15 year period, the benefits were outstanding. For each $1,000 invested in 1940, $3,000,000 was the total return by the 1990's. Investing more cautiously in the large companies of the S&P 500, for instance, our $1,000 would have grown to almost a $1,000,00 by 2000. Yes, the lines are not perfectly straight, but growing $500 a month to $1,000,000 is definitely worth the ups and downs. Inflation is designated by the bottom line here. Putting all our money in a bank CD would accumulate at a rate represented by a line near that bottom line.

Of course, these different rates of wealth accumulation assume two important factors—NO taxes and LOW costs. We have eliminated the first killer of wealth—TAXES—by using a tax-FREE trust account. Costs of the investment type we use can also kill your total accumulations. The whole financial industry is built on the extraction of these costs from the accounts of investors. We must use low-cost stock funds to have a *Tax-FREE Retirement*.

Summary: Set up automatic monthly contributions for no interruptions.

One of the most difficult parts of building wealth is sticking with the program. If we put our monthly contributions on automatic, we will have no interruptions. If we instruct our trustee to debit our savings or checking account every month, we have a high probability of meeting our goals over time. We set it and forget it. We forget we are investing in our future and thus we actually create one. What an irony! Reward comes to the patient person! This is the *Lazy Person's Way to Wealth.*

$2,000 Annual Stock Market Investment 1950- '70- '80- '90- 2012

Year	Returns	Balance	Balance	Balance	Balance
		$2,000			
1950	31%	$2,620			
1951	24%	$5,729			
1952	18%	$9,120			
1953	-1%	$11,009			
1954	52%	$19,773			
1955	31%	$28,523			
1956	5%	$32,049			
1957	-11%	$30,304			
1958	43%	$46,194			
1959	12%	$53,978			
1960	1%	$56,538			
1961	26%	$73,757			
1962	-8%	$69,697			
1963	24%	$88,904			
1964	16%	$105,449			
1965	12%	$120,342			
1966	-10%	$110,108			
1967	24%	$139,014			
1968	11%	$156,526			
1969	-8%	$145,844	2,000		
1970	4%	$153,757	2,080		
1971	14%	$177,563	4,651		
1972	19%	$213,681	7,915		
1973	-14%	$185,485	8,527		
1974	-26%	$138,739	7,790		
1975	37%	$192,813	13,412		
1976	24%	$241,568	19,111		
1977	-8%	$224,082	19,422		
1978	6%	$239,647	22,707		
1979	18%	$285,144	29,155	2,000	
1980	32%	$379,030	41,124	2,640	
1981	-5%	$361,978	40,968	4,408	
1982	22%	$444,053	52,421	7,818	
1983	21%	$539,724	65,850	11,879	
1984	6%	$574,228	71,921	14,712	
1985	32%	$760,621	97,575	22,060	
1986	19%	$907,519	118,494	28,632	
1987	5%	$954,995	126,519	32,163	
1988	17%	$1,119,684	150,367	39,971	
1989	32%	$1,480,623	201,125	55,402	2,000
1990	-3%	$1,438,144	197,031	55,680	1,940
1991	31%	$1,886,589	260,731	75,560	5,161
1992	8%	$2,039,676	283,749	83,765	7,734
1993	10%	$2,245,843	314,324	94,342	10,708
1994	2%	$2,292,800	322,651	98,268	12,962
1995	38%	$3,166,824	448,018	138,370	20,647
1996	23%	$3,897,654	553,522	172,656	27,856
1997	33%	$5,186,540	738,844	232,292	39,709
1998	28%	$6,641,331	948,281	299,894	53,387
1999	21%	$8,038,430	1,149,839	365,291	67,019
2000	-9%	$7,316,791	1,048,174	334,235	62,807
2001	-12%	$6,447,855	925,203	296,223	57,095
2002	-22%	$5,024,437	722,291	232,316	46,035
2003	29%	$6,459,474	930,787	301,119	61,730
2004	11%	$7,164,483	1,034,274	336,099	70,664
2005	5%	$7,512,677	1,084,540	352,433	74,098
2006	15%	$8,694,884	1,259,259	412,409	90,450
2007	5%	$9,163,538	1,327,133	434,638	95,325
2008	-39%	$5,601,431	813,388	268,074	60,754
2009	27%	$7,116,358	952,155	342,993	79,699
2010	15%	$8,186,112	1,097,278	396,742	93,954
2011	2%	$8,347,378	1,118,894	404,558	95,805
2012	16%	$9,666,264	1,295,679	468,478	110,942
Avg.	12%	12%	11%	13%	10%

Ibbotson Associates **Stocks average 11.4% per year, bonds 5%, CDs 3%.** Stocks have gone up as much as 54% and as low as –43% in 1 year, up to 28% or down to –12% in 5 years, up 20% or down 0% in 10 years, up 18% or up 3% in 20 years. Short term bonds have gone up 14% or up 0% in 1 year, up 11% or up 0% in 5 years, up 9% or up 0% in 10 years, up 10% or up 1% in 20 years.

5

Use low-cost mutual funds only

"In every single time period and data point tested,
***low-cost* funds beat high-cost funds."**

According to this unbiased <u>Morningstar</u> study, low-cost funds always beat high-cost funds. However, the myth of Wall Street is that you must pay more for good performance. Not true. We all know that in most groceries' prices, paying more (for packaging and TV commercials) does not guarantee a better product.

The **best predictor** of your investing and wealth-building success is low cost funds. It is common sense that there are just too many variables in the success of growing companies' stocks for anyone to be able to pick them in advance consistently. A low-cost stock mutual fund provides the best chance of maximizing our accumulations as the market leaders change over time.

Contrary to Wall Street's hype, it does not matter which stocks are rising or falling at any given time. If our account holds a broad representation of stocks and our investment costs are low, we will benefit over the long haul. We own them all!

Since the annual returns of stock funds have averaged 10-12% over time, we want to pick the lowest cost mutual fund available. A stock fund that reflects the overall market is called an index fund. This kind of fund explained below costs only 0.07% ($7 per $10,000). Our account will compound at or near the 10-12% over time since the costs are low compared to ones that charge 1-3%. If we use the high-cost stock funds, we will earn 7-9% over time. These funds pay managers high salaries with expensive bonuses. The fund owners and sales staff are paid well also. This is the cash cow of Wall Street.

The chart below makes it clear. Over time, the costs we pay each year will cut our total accumulation by a THIRD or more. Instead of compounding at 10-12% annually on average, some people give up 1-3% of the earnings on their money to the middle person. They end up with less.

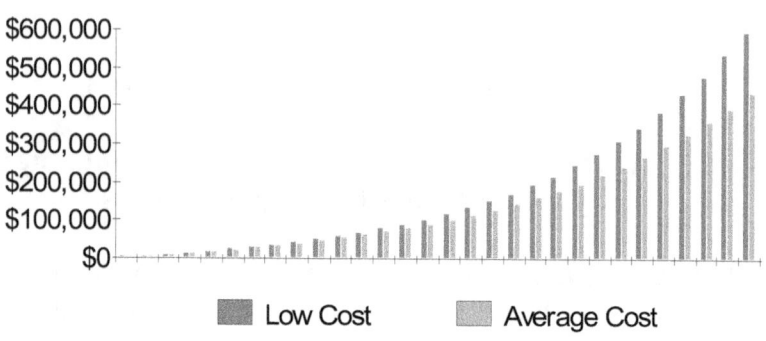

Cost Matters: 0.19% v 1.68%

Low Cost   Average Cost

Wall Street says that we can earn more by paying a star manager to pick the right stocks on an ongoing basis. The money "experts" say we get what we pay for and a proven stock-picking manager will overcome the extra costs and make more for us.

The reality is that this **myth has been proven wrong**. The lowest cost funds don't pay a star manager and owner big bucks but come out ahead over time. There are simply too many variables for anyone or computer program to pick the winning stocks all the time. Some of the lowest cost funds are called index funds. When we buy an market index, we are buying a piece of many companies. This gives us the same annual returns as the overall market over time. We pay tiny expenses. *We keep more*!

Many studies have proven that index funds beat funds run by stock pickers most of the time. Low-cost index funds beat 86% of funds with a stock-picking manager. *BusinessWeek* Apr 2009. http://www.businessweek.com/investing/insights/blog/archives/2009/04/where_have_all.html.

When we investigate the experiences of the best money managers in the world, we find they recommend index funds to most people who invest as silent partners. Here are their statements:

Warren Buffett is probably history's greatest investor, in terms of results with $44 BILLION ($44 thousand million dollars) so far. He buys *companies* that provide valuable services to a great number of people. His company owns parts of Coke, GEICO, Fruit of the Loom, Benjamin Moore, Acme Bricks, Burlington Northern, etc. berkshirehathaway.com/

He told Reuters: "A very low-cost index is going to beat a majority of the amateur-managed money or professionally-managed money."

Compare the odds of selecting the correct mutual fund. A fund's chance of beating the market in EACH year is 3 out of 100. nytimes.com/2009/02/22/your-money/stocks-and-bonds/22stra.html

Peter Lynch, brilliant manager, Magellan Fund "…you'd be just as well off if you'd invested in the S&P 500." *One Up on Wall Street*, 1989, p. 240.

Jonathan Clements, formerly *The Wall Street Journal*
"Most people can do it themselves. ... By indexing, you don't just ensure that you will do better than most other investors. You will also enjoy the advantage of 'relative certainty.' . . . For most investors, Vanguard will be the place to go." *You've Lost It, Now What? How to beat the bear market and still retire on time*, 2003, p. 62, 70.

Charles D. Ellis, money managers' consultant
"The premise . . . that professional investment managers *can* beat the market . . . appears to be false. It is a loser's game. ... clients would have done better in a market fund." Returns are "splendidly predictable—on average and over time." *Investment Policy, How to Win the Loser's Game*, 1985, p. 5, 20, 34.

Jane Bryant Quinn, consumer advisor
"I'm a longtime booster of index mutual funds. These funds follow the market as a whole. Tons of research has shown that most money managers don't beat the markets they invest in, after costs. Maybe your own stocks or funds have excelled in the past couple of years. But in most cases, you've also been taking extra risk. The odds of superior performance are against you, in the long run. Indexing puts the odds on your side." *Los Angeles Business Journal*, May 8, 2000

<u>Charles Schwab</u> founder, discount broker
"I put my money where my mouth is: most of the mutual fund investments I have are in index funds, approximately 75%. My <u>core investments</u> are <u>index funds</u>. Experienced investors have discovered that in any given year, on average, only 20 to 30 percent of mutual funds outperform the market. That is why I recommend index funds…"
Mr. Schwab tells of one of his friends who owned many well-run funds. After keeping track of all the dividends, taxes, reinvestments tax basis and statements, he found he earned the same return as the index of these funds. After selling them all, he bought the index fund. He has "what he wanted in the first place: diversification, tax advantages, one statement, and lower expenses." *Guide to Financial Independence*, 1998, pp. 90, 103, 111.

<u>Motley Fool,</u> Internet site about investing
"Almost **everything** that you will ever read about mutual funds beyond, "Buy an <u>index fund.</u>" is superfluous to your long-term success in investing in mutual funds." <u>Fool.com.</u>

<u>Walter Updegrave</u>, senior editor, *Money*
"Mutual fund picking would be easier if there was one you could count on to outperform 70% or so of its competitors over long stretches of a decade or more. It's called an <u>index fund</u>. Although less than 10% of investors own an index fund, they are "<u>one of the best-kept secrets" on Wall Street</u>. My unabashed aim is to convince you to put at least a part of your money into one or more of these funds. You have a far less than a 50% chance of beating the market…. I strongly recommend that you make index funds your primary holding…." *The Right Way to Invest in Mutual Funds*, 1996, p 189-194.

<u>Andrew Tobias</u>, financial writer
"Scrimp and save, putting whatever you can into no-load, low-expense stock market <u>index funds</u>, both U.S. and foreign. You will do better than 80% of your friends and neighbors." *My Vast Fortune*, 1997, p. 158.

There are many books written on the subject of index and "managed" funds. If you wish to vanquish the hype and understand investing, skim *A Random Walk Down Wall Street* by Princeton University's Burton Malkiel. Here are the reasons why smart insiders use low-cost funds:

1. Both stock and bond index funds provide better returns than 86% of managed funds for periods greater than 10 years.
2. You earn more because you pay lower costs and taxes.
3. Low-cost funds build greater wealth over time.
4. Low-cost funds can be less volatile because they reflect whole sectors of the market.
5. Low-cost funds offer better diversification.
6. You know what you are paying for. No high-salary managers.
7. Low-cost funds don't require you to hope the manager will predict the future correctly. The odds of doing it are 1 in 15,000 each year separately. Over time, all funds provide average returns minus their costs.
8. Low-cost funds are easy to buy.

> "Professional money management is a gigantic rip-off."
> Bill Gross, star bond manager, *Everything You've Heard About Investing is Wrong*

Summary of many studies about index investing

First, fund managers try to predict the future of the market when they buy and sell securities in their funds. There is no proof this can be done well over time. Yesterday's winners are usually tomorrow's losers. The AVERAGE market return has been 10-12%, so a few managers will beat the average by luck—Just not the same ones every year. nytimes.com/2008/07/13/business/13stra.html
Second, the costs of the manager, their staff and operations must be paid for by you whether or not they earn you a dime. It is always better to pay as little as possible for the same performance. Costs can take 33% of your returns over time. Surprisingly, while the stock index rose 9%, investors with high paid managers averaged only **2.56%** annually from 1990-2010 (QAIB). DALBARinc.com.
Third, high cost managers get paid for increasing the size of their funds, not for making you rich. Bringing in more money is a full-

time job. It is expensive to market the funds given that there are now thousands available. It is inevitable that popular funds will grow until they produce average returns with high expenses. Managers want to be rich, not right.

Fourth, there is much less chance of you being treated poorly by fund management if the structure and governance are customer-oriented like Vanguard's and TIAA-CREF's are.

Fifth, many professional managers, pension funds, and Wall Street insiders place their core assets in low-cost index funds.

Summary: Use low-cost mutual funds only.

The best predictor of the success of a mutual fund is its cost. Why pay more than you have to? Usually the least expensive funds that match market averages beat the more expensive managed funds. Low-cost market index funds buy all the securities represented in a broad market. The goal of an index fund is to match its market. Low-cost index funds have provided returns that beat 80-90% of managed funds over the long-term. No manager has been able to predict the future so the returns regress to the mean—the 10%-12%. Wealthy people bet on the averages not the long shot. They don't like to lose value. The patient investor is rewarded in the long run. This is the *Lazy Person's Way to Wealth.*

"In every single time period and data point tested, low-cost funds beat high-cost funds."

6

Buy groups of stocks of growing companies worldwide

If we want to have $1,000,000 for tax-FREE income, we need a way to make it happen—a strategy. To be able to have a nest egg of $1 million requires that we know how and where to invest, invest regularly, invest properly, monitor accumulations along the way, and get help when we need it. We need a clear plan that takes only one hour to set up and only one hour per year to manage. Complicated plans just don't work for most people. Complicated strategies cost more to execute.

Picking *individual* stocks as a strategy is not likely to work for us. Professional managers and day traders have had limited success **over time**, unless they have <u>insider information</u>. Our strategy is to build wealth as a **silent partner** in growing global companies. Since it is unlikely that we (or anyone else) will be able to pick the next 'Apple,' we must invest in a large group of firms. We do not need to fear picking the wrong one or picking one at the wrong time. As the founder of the largest mutual fund firm, John Bogle, says: "Don't look for the needle. Buy the haystack."

This is contrary to the myth of Wall Street 'professionals.' They make their living claiming to find the needle every year and we pay the price. Professionals promise that they can find the next big one and we pay them well because we want to be rich. But....

Like the lottery, we kid ourselves into thinking that "someone has to win, why not me." We don't believe we are wasting our money even though our rational mind knows that our chance of winning is low. Managed funds don't beat the market most of the time. The odds are like those of a lottery—18 million to 1. Like the lottery, when we invest in a managed fund to "beat the market" we don't count up the costs of the "tickets." We may buy $25 worth of tickets a week and end up winning $1,000 in a year. We spent $1,200 for $1,000.

In the same manner, a mutual fund manager advertises that their fund has "beaten" the market and so we pay 1-3% of our assets every year. Over time we find that while the stock market index rose 9% from 1990-2010, we earned only 2.56% annually. This is what happened to retail investors according to Dalbar's QAIB recent study. DALBARinc.com

Some of us keep switching to the 'hot' funds according to the advertising we see every month. Some are always chasing the last successful mutual fund. Some buy the fund at the high point because they want the winner. They sell the fund when it falls and they want the next high flier. Over time they never earn the return promised by the manager.

In this way, activity can take 40% of their returns over time. Each time they sell and buy, they give up earnings and perhaps part of their money if they use a sales person charging 5%. Even if they stay with one managed mutual fund that has annual fees of 1-3%, they are killing the miracle of compounding.

Using the compounding calculator, we can see that our accumulation drops to $0.7 million if we earn 10.5% instead of 11.8% annually. We could have $1 million in about 30 years at 11.6% using low-cost funds, no tax and no trading. http://www.moneychimp.com/calculator/compound_interest_calcul ator.htm

Another Wall Street myth is that investing in market index funds will produce **only** average (mediocre) returns. It is true that the returns will be close to the returns of the market. However, historically the market returns are the ones that are somewhat predictable. Investing in companies inside an index provides no guaranteed return but the average returns have held steady since the 1930s when they started keeping records.

Wall Street's history is littered with strategies that were said to beat the market. The brilliant stock pickers have also come and gone. Today, though, which one of the new ones are we going to invest with? No one knows. The ONLY thing we really know is that the averages of broad market indexes have produced 10-12% on average each year. See page 32.

For example, some of my clients use these Vanguard mutual funds which have earned over 11% for a long time. Of course, there is no guarantee of future returns, but they have all done fairly well. Most started with the 500 Index and added companies in the Energy, Health and International sectors. These 10 funds have done well over time. Many investors pick Vanguard funds because the funds are well run at cost. No "bells and whistles." No expensive managers and overhead. No owner taking profits from our investment returns, even when there are none.

1 Year Return*	Fund	Long-term Return*	Longevity
17.82%	500 Index	10.55%	since 1976
-0.67%	Energy	12.43%	since 1984
13.08%	Extended Market	10.18%	since 1987
13.51%	Health	16.32%	since 1984
-1.14%	International Growth	10.54%	since 1981
12.74%	PRIMECAP	12.88%	since 1984
14.48%	Small Cap Index	10.36%	since 1960
13.27%	Wellesley Income	10.20%	since 1970
16.31%	Windsor	11.11%	since 1958
18.39%	Windsor II	10.41%	since 1985
11.78%	Average	11.50%	

*Average Annual Returns as of 8/31/12.

My clients are patient long-term investors, not speculators. They believe that investments in low-cost funds (index and team-managed) are their best chance of reaching their goals. They have been rewarded for that belief. Vanguard has many low-cost funds and their customer service is better than most funds provide.

Remember, we are investing for the long-term. Most pension funds are invested in stock and bond indexes. Even though the market fell 22% in 2002 and jumped 29% in 2003, the average was still holding. Average returns mean we do not suffer the lowest lows nor the highest highs. Returns regress to the mean: 10-12%.

Most of the largest growing companies in the world are held by these funds. Large US firms are now earning at least **half of their profits overseas** so we are benefiting from growth around the world. This is important because we don't want to miss important earnings progress as the developing nations like China and India expand their economies.

We don't know exactly which companies will be winners so we participate in all of them. We want to own some smaller growing companies too. If they become successful, they will move to the large company funds. We are exposed to almost all areas of the global economy by buying shares of these mutual funds at the lowest cost. We suffer the ups and downs of the markets just like every investor. However, we see that some funds do better at certain times while others do worse. Together we see clients hitting their goal of 10-12% average annual returns.

This type of investing has the greatest chance of avoiding severe swings in the balance of our accumulation. This type of strategy—investing in different types and sizes of companies in different sectors around the world—is called Modern Portfolio Theory. It is probably the best way to assure you of predictable retirement income too.

Modern Portfolio Theory

Some clients use the MPT strategy to control risk while increasing returns. MPT (Moneychimp.com/articles/risk/riskintro.htm) holds that if we put our eggs in different baskets of assets that grow at different times, then the value of all our 'eggs' grows with fewer ups and downs. We can manage the ups and downs of equity funds by buying different ones over time. Higher risk assets are small caps, REITs and foreign stocks. This strategy earns 10-12% with 30% less volatility.

Members assemble asset classes (see callan.com/research/download/?file=periodic/free/457.pdf) that fit their risk-reward tastes. According to this Nobel Prize-winning strategy moneychimp.com/articles/risk/portfolio.htm, a high return asset with a low correlation to other assets in the portfolio can actually reduce the volatility of the whole. It may be possible to earn high returns with less risk **overall** as each asset goes up and down at different times. See the example at fool.com/personal-finance/retirement/2007/03/06/5-steps-to-salvage-your-retirement.aspx.

The past provides only PROBABLE futures. But isn't $1,000,000 (plus or minus $100,000) better than $150,000. Your $250/$500-per-month deposit in the bank for about 30 years will be worth about $150,000 after tax compared with about $1 million from stock investing with no tax. Every investor would be better off with $1 million (+/- $100,000) than $150,000 from a bank.

When clients begin investing, they cannot buy all 10 Vanguard funds at once with $500 (couple) per month. Vanguard has minimums on all funds so they can keep their expenses low for everyone. They start with $1,000 in the STAR fund.

There are two ways to start our **Wealth Reserve**™.

The easiest way is to save $500 a month in our savings account until we have the $1,000 minimum for Vanguard's entry fund: STAR #56. We can open the Roth IRA by phone or online: STAR minimum is $1,000. Most Vanguard funds need $3,000 to start. We can keep contributing to this index fund until we have $3,000 for the 500 Index and then $3,000 for the Extended Market funds. Vanguard is at 800.551.8631. STAR has returned 9.5% since 1985.

The second way to begin is to open a Roth IRA at TIAA-CREF, the world's largest pension company, primarily for educational and research institutions. Low expenses and low initial contributions make TIAA-CREF an organization we can stay with for life. TIAA-CREF 800.842.2888.

At TIAA-CREF.org, we can make application and begin immediately with an automatic monthly contribution of $100 or more from our bank account. We can follow how the assets grow by themselves. TIAA-CREF has two funds that provide us with the diversity of companies worldwide: TIAA-CREF Equity Index and TIAA International Equity.

Request a *prospectus* (owner's manual) for each fund you will be using at Vanguard or TIAA-CREF. Both mutual fund firms have experienced salaried representatives that provide accurate information about accounts and funds. Both offer low-cost index funds that hold a broad representation of the market returns of 10-12%. This is a building block to accumulating wealth.

Both firms are focused on you, not on profits.

Summary: Buy mutual fund shares (groups of stocks of growing companies worldwide).

This strategy provides long-term returns of 10-12% annually on average with the benefit of avoiding single company or industry failures. It provides exposure to new growth potential around the world with less risk than holding one company, one sector, or one country. *Ten funds provide income, growth and diversification.*

This is the Lazy Person's Way to Wealth.

It is the amount we KEEP that matters!

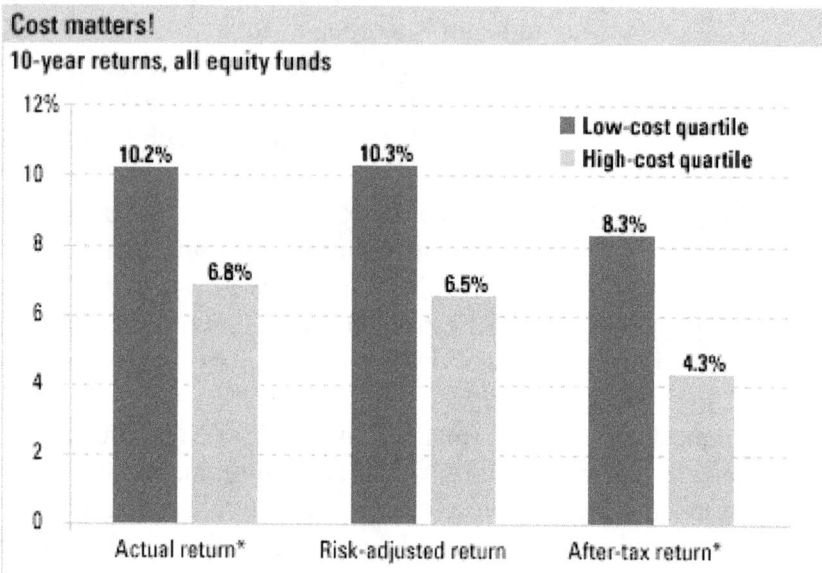

Cost matters!

10-year returns, all equity funds

*Source: Morningstar avg. ann. returns for 10 yrs ended 8/03.

7

Spend less than you earn

We need to find at least $250 per month to invest in order to build our **Wealth Reserve**™. We can build wealth by following the strategy outlined in the previous chapters, but we need to have at least $250 available in the first place. In my experience, it doesn't matter how much people earn, most say they don't have the $250 a month to invest for their future. "Today is hard enough," they complain.

Yes, that may well be, but if we don't find the $250-$500 we won't have a very happy tomorrow. We have to go back to our goal. We want to build wealth: accumulating $1,000,000 over time. Based on the way wealth compounds, we need to identify at least $250 a month on a permanent basis. We need to be consistent in investing for the miracle of compounding to work.

'Budget' is a dirty word so we won't use it. No one wants to be restricted in their spending. Even the people who know they are wasting $100 a month on the lottery, still play. I know it satisfies an immediate-riches fantasy. I know because I used to play every week like many others who never saw the **power of compounding**.

I want to explain how we can find the $250 a month to invest from a different perspective. If we are going to spend all of our income, we need to adopt a "spending plan" with the $250-$500 a month for investment included in it. Otherwise, we won't accumulate $1,000,000. Even if we don't have 30 years or so, our $500 could grow to a significant sum.

A spending plan is just a way to set priorities for our regular spending. During our working lives, we earn about $1.5 to $2.5 million. We can accumulate another $1 million to accomplish all that we want to do in life by using just 10 percent of that income to buy assets that "grow by themselves."

Using a Spending Plan is **like brushing your teeth**—it's a habit that isn't that difficult to learn—then it is automatic. If we want our plan to become a habit, we have to practice it. If we consciously spend our income on those items on our priority list, we can't fail to develop the habit. We are teaching ourselves that we can have whatever we want, in time. We are not saying "no" to that desire. We are saying put it on our list. We will get what we want eventually.

First, our Spending Plan must include what we need to function. Our future is part of our immediate needs in the sense that if we don't prepare now, we won't have the future we want. Again, building a $1,000,000 **Wealth Reserve**™ is a lifelong process and requires making a commitment. Like building a business, it takes planning and following the steps we talked about so far.

There are a number of ways to identify the $500 a month we need to build our future. Some clients include the $500 in their automatic bill payment or have the trustee debit their account automatically. The contribution is just another bill like rent, mortgage, utilities, car payment, cable, phone, etc. They live on the balance of their income.

Others set up family goals and decide to put a certain amount in a separate account for each goal. In this way, they keep the wealth building process in the forefront of their monthly bill payments ritual. Others make investing automatic—out of sight.

Whatever way works for you. The important part is changing the status of wealth-building from a vague future to a monthly priority. Making it automatic assures you that you will succeed.

Most clients find that the easiest way is to set up an automatic debit of their checking account by the trustee at the time of the application for the Roth IRA. If we are using a Roth 401k or other employer account, we set up the retirement account with automatic contributions.

The Spending Plan idea works for all types of goals: college fund, emergency fund, vacation fund, new car fund, business start-up fund, whatever we decide to put at the top of our list of priorities. If we don't have this list, we can make one easily.

Clients who are successful have made written plans in some form or other. They have some idea of how much they will need at some time in the future. For short-term goals we can use our savings account but for long-term (5 years) goals we need to use higher return mutual funds. Many clients have trouble deciding which investment to use for each goal.

I explained the chart we displayed on page 12 above. Stock mutual funds are the investment of choice for any long-term accumulation goal. As per the chart, annual returns of 10-12% are the norm for any accumulation over 10-15 years. Once we build up a sizable balance in a long-term account, we can "borrow" from ourselves for short-term needs as long as we pay ourselves back.

Thus, clients have used their long-term accumulation **Wealth Reserve**™ for vacations, cars, appliances, emergencies, etc. This works if they pay themselves back. The **Wealth Reserve**™ is set up as a Roth IRA so the *contributions* are not taxed when used before age 59.5. After that age, there are no taxes at all—NEVER. However, to meet our long-term goals, we have to pay ourselves back quickly to take advantage of compounding.

Another benefit of using a Spending Plan is that we become focused on how we spend our money. We are more inclined to buy only what we need. For most of us, when we shop for groceries, we seek to get the most for our money by shopping for discounts and by buying in bulk. In the last ten years, the financial services industry has started to offer better values on products. We can avoid overpaying the middle people and buying products we really don't need. We can buy direct, without the middle person.

How do we know. The Insiders Guides provide an easy way to save $3,000 or more on financial products we already use. There are buyer's Guides for each specific area. We review some of the ways to find $250 in savings in the next chapter.

Summary: Spend less than you earn.

We can't build wealth by spending more than we earn. Building wealth takes patience and commitment to investing every month. The *Lazy Person's Way to Wealth* does not NOT require you to be disciplined. We let the trustee debit the $250-$500 every month so we can't fail to create our tax-FREE $1,000,000.

Are you paying too much?

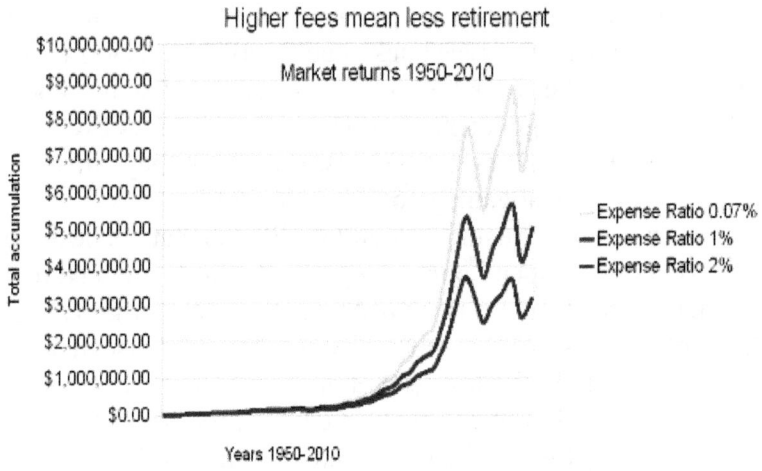

8

Buy only the services/products you need—no "bells and whistles"

It is easy to build wealth if we already have a pile of money. It takes 7-9 years to accumulate $1 million if we already have $500,000. But how do we capture that first $500,000, that $250,000, or even that first $50,000? It comes from buying assets that 'grow by themselves.' It takes time and the easiest way to make sure we reach our goal is to make our monthly contributions automatic.

But where do we get the $250 or more? The best way is to "REDIRECT" the **cash we already spend** on things we really don't need or can buy for less.

Monthly	Accumulation at 12% per year									
	5	10	15	20	25	30	35	40	45	50
$100	$8,167	$23,004	$49,958	$98,925	$187,884	$349,496	$643,095	$1,176,477	$2,145,469	$3,905,834
$200	$16,334	$46,008	$99,916	$197,850	$375,768	$698,992	$1,286,190	$2,352,954	$4,290,938	$7,811,668
$300	$24,501	$69,012	$149,874	$296,775	$563,652	$1,048,488	$1,929,285	$3,529,431	$6,436,408	$11,717,502
$500	$40,835	$115,020	$249,790	$494,625	$939,420	$1,747,480	$3,215,475	$5,882,385	$10,727,346	$19,529,169

While working with clients, I have found that most of us waste $3,000 or more each year on financial services. We can stop paying for services we don't need. This takes a little thought and questioning on our part, but in reality it is the same process as buying any commodity. When we buy groceries, do we buy the house brand or the one on sale or the one we see advertised? On a little bigger scale, do we buy the new car advertised with a new "push" starter as opposed to a used car with a key? Do we pay an extra $1000 to buy the one with a PC screen to tell us where to go or just use a map. The difference between paying full price for a new car and a 3-year-old model with fewer gadgets can be 40% or more. When we put our future on top of our priority list, we can REDIRECT the savings to a more worthwhile purpose.

It is the same with financial services. Most of us are not used to shopping for insurance, mutual funds, banking and mortgages. So we don't. We are operating under the mythology of Wall Street —'professionals' say we need them to help guide us, for a price. **But we don't need them anymore**. The world has changed.

Let's take some examples of <u>annual savings</u>:

Auto insurance: save $400 or more EVERY year by changing/dropping some extras we don't need.

Home insurance: save $200 or more EVERY year by changing one limit.

Life insurance: save $1,000 or more EVERY year by using direct to consumer insurer and low-cost term.

Mutual funds: save $2-3,000 EVERY year by using a low-cost provider.

Banking: save $120 EVERY year by using a low-cost provider of the benefits we usually use.

Mortgage: save $2,000 on closings and lower interest rates.

Investments: earn 15-30% guaranteed just by paying off credit cards too.

Using the Insiders' Guides put together by Dan Keppel in his book *The Insiders' Guides to Buying Discount Financial Services: Buy Direct and Save $3,000 Every Year,* we can REDIRECT the $250 a month without having to give up anything important. We don't need to 'tighten our belts' or make a budget. We can give up things we would not benefit from anyway.

Dan gave me a number of testimonials from people who have told him about their experience using the Guides.

George B. New York:
"I saved $1,356 on my vehicle insurance using your Insider's Guide to Vehicle Insurance. I saved by using some of your Insiders' 'tricks of the trade' like dropping the extras that I already had."

John D. New York:
"I canceled my life insurance and used the money to buy the mutual funds. You were right. I didn't need the insurance anymore. My kids are all grown. My new wife and I invest as much as we can now. Your Guide to 'Living' Insurance is a great way to look at our insurance needs."

Mark K. Ohio:
"I had no idea how to invest in the 401k that my new job offered. I have not been disappointed with the mutual funds suggested by other members. I saved about a $1,000 by transferring my old 401k mutual funds to the low-cost funds in your Guide. When I sold my primary residence in 2004, I followed members' advice with the gains. I use all your Guides to help me save more for my retirement since I got a late start. Thanks."

Dan has a great example of the big savings we can expect by shopping for insurance. Dan found that people usually pick name brands instead of shopping for services they need. Companies spend a lot for TV advertising and gimmicks that cost you.

Example:

MetLife charged $983 for a $300,000 30-year **term policy**. This same $300,000 benefit was sold by Savings Bank Life Insurance for $384 a year. Their financial strength ratings are A+ and their underwriting requirements are the same. The difference, $599, over 30 years is $17,970. If invested, this difference can add $175,000 to OUR **Wealth Reserve**™.

Most people are amazed at the difference a little research and shopping can accomplish. Even if we did not have Dan's Guides, a search of the Internet would reveal several portals that quote rates. Unfortunately, most people don't take the time to shop or don't know exactly what they need. The Guides help us make the decision of where to shop and what to buy.

Summary: Buy only the services you need—no "bells and whistles."

Buying only what we need in every financial service area will provide the cash for contributions to your wealth. Taking the time to shop in each area of our expenses helps us make our future happen. Shopping for an hour can add $175,000 to our account. Yes, it is worth it!

This is the *Lazy Person's Way to Wealth.*

The Roth IRA Rules

Contributions:

$5,500 ($6,500 over age 50) each year
Income under $127,000 (2013) single
married $188,000 (2013)

Distributions:

Tax-FREE for contributions.
And Tax-FREE for earnings if
Over age 591/2,
Account open 5 years,
Earnings are taxable if under age, unless
Disabled, or
First home ($10,000), or
Death

Bonus:

Account can grow tax-FREE for life
Distribution rules don't apply
Heirs don't pay income tax
Account has no maximum

Check with your tax preparer
www.IRS.gov/pub/irs-pdf/p590.pdf

9

Manage the account only once a year

We continue to make more money when *snoring* than when active.

Warren Buffett, Berkshirehathaway.com/

This is the advice of the most successful investor of our day. He is making it clear that we should NOT touch our investments very often. Contrary to the advice of the Wall Street 'professionals,' he leaves his assets alone to compound over time. He does not follow the 'hot' investment of the day. He buys the stock of growing companies around the world. He has held some investments for over 40 years—Coke, GEICO, Disney, Wells Fargo, Gillette, etc.

Our emotions tell us to sell when our account balance goes down. We want to buy the next big investment to make up for previous losses. This is why we have a hard time following Buffett's advice. However, the emotions that cause us to be bad investors are what we can control—not the stock price of growing companies worldwide. Patience is a habit we can learn.

Our contributions to our **Wealth Reserve**™ need to be automatic so we buy more shares when the market is down and less when it is up. This helps us control our emotions. When the market is down, we need to look at the line graph on page 16. We don't know when the market will be up or down but we see that if we sell, we may miss the next advance. This is why we have to remember Warren Buffett's advice and hold on to stocks. In fact, Mr Buffett says "**our favorite holding period is forever.**" http://www.berkshirehathaway.com/letters/1988.html

When we own a broad cross-section of the market, we really don't have to worry about buying and selling our mutual funds. There is no better investment for the long term. Besides, what would we buy if we sold? We have seen that stocks are the safest investment for periods over 10 years. Patience is profitable.

We believe that the only way to avoid bad investment decisions is to NOT make any investment decisions in haste. Stick with the idea that we only have to look at our tax-FREE account once a year. At that time, I make sure I am making contributions to the specific mutual fund I need to build in order to keep them equally funded. I don't sell because there is no safer investment.

For instance, when I first started investing, I used the 500 Index. After I had accumulated enough to buy the Extended Market, I sold shares of 500 Index ($3,000) and bought it. I kept investing into the 500 Index until I had the minimum for the next one on the list. I repeated this pattern until I had the minimum in each. Then I picked one to add $250 a month for one year. The next year, I did the same until I completed the list again and again.

Today, I am still making contributions using the same rotation. Once a year, I compare the total account balance to where I think it should be. I note what happened during the year for any one fund. I go to the Vanguard site and read about that fund. Do I need to make a change? No, usually I don't. I use the 10 funds listed above. They have done well consistently over the years.

Notice that when we buy each fund at first, we have to sell shares in the 500 Index to do so. Because we are using a Roth IRA, there is no tax on this sale if the share price has gone up. Also, each year, our dividends are re-invested without paying tax on that income. This is part of the miracle of compounding. Our account is growing without taxes each year. Any other non-retirement account would be diminished by the tax paid each year.

There is no need to sell funds that have done well in order to re-balance the 10 funds' balances equally. Most of the research shows that re-balancing each year does not change the long-term outcome of the whole portfolio. Some clients use their contributions each year to add to the fund that has grown the **least**. However, as each fund becomes larger, the effect of adding contributions becomes smaller over time.

When we have to sell shares to meet an emergency or avoid interest payments by using cash for large ticket items, we may sell shares in each fund by equal dollar amounts. This is a better strategy than selling shares in only one fund since we don't know which fund may recover the fastest going forward. In the same way as accumulating shares, we need to reimburse our account for the amount used. It is very desirable to also continue to make contributions at the regular rate—$250-$500 per month. This way we are assured of catching up to our position as we reach our goal.

However, we found that after accumulating a large proportion of our goal, making contributions did not seem to matter to the outcome. For instance, our client whose account is shown on page 22 took $25,000 for a used luxury car in the year the account hit over half a million. He also stopped making contributions. His account total did not suffer long term.

Actually this client redirected his $250 monthly contribution to his grandchild's **Wealth Reserve**™ so that they might have a financial foundation all their life. If he keeps giving this $3,000 a year to his offspring for 40 years, they could have $2,000,000 by age 50. The grandchild "earns" $3,000 a year doing odd jobs for him. Learn more about this "Gift of a Lifetime" in Dan Keppel's book, amazon.com/Give-your-Grandchild-2,000,000-Lifetime/.

Summary: Manage the account only once a year.

Our tax-FREE retirement income account does not require us to hire an advisor to manage it. Advisors do not know what the future holds anymore than we do so paying them 1-3% each year just reduces our annual returns. Their fees/charges can take up to 40% of our total accumulations over time. We are investing for the long term and there is proof that switching from one fund to another during the year only hurts our results. As we add more contributions, we can rotate through each fund. The less we tamper with our fund balances the better our experience will be. Remember, we are silent partners in growing businesses around the world.
This is the *Lazy Person's Way to Wealth.*

Your Action Plan
This is the *Lazy Person's Way to Wealth.*
This week:
Goal

_____

_____

This month:
Goal

_____

_____

_____

_____

This year:
Goals

_____

_____

_____

_____

_____

_____

_____

_____

_____

_____

_____

_____

10

Take $80,000 tax-FREE income each year in retirement

We have used the 10 steps of building wealth. We have learned to be patient and accumulate $1,000,000 or more. We have paid back any amounts that we borrowed to pay cash for large purchases. We have been fortunate that the historical averages of market returns have produced the accumulations we set as our goals.

NOW WHAT?

Now we can take $80,000 out of the account each year and pay no income taxes. As of 2012, most states follow the IRS code on our **Wealth Reserve**™, a Roth IRA—§ 408 trust account. No state tax. http://www.irs.gov/retirement/article/0,,id=137307,00.html

Some clients have moved some of their accumulations into tax-FREE bond funds in order to provide a monthly credit into their checking account for their regular expenses. They created a retirement spending plan that assured them of that monthly income of a fixed dollar amount with this Guide. amazon.com/Your-Retirement-Spending-Plan-enough

We have to create our $1,000,000 nest egg in order to provide the same buying power as we have today because of inflation. I am assuming that most families will need at least $40,000 (current dollars) a year to live on in retirement. We don't know what will happen to Social Security by 2037. We don't know what employer pensions might look like by then. I am assuming that inflation will continue at a 3% rate. It might be more or less. I have no idea. However, we must prepare for inflation.

At 3%, inflation will make the goods we now buy for $40,000 cost about $80,000. This is not exact. I don't know what will happen in 30 days let alone 30 years. If Social Security or employer pensions can provide our basic income, that is fine. But we don't want to count on them. We need to grow our accounts.

I am using $40,000 as a basic needs income because that has been my experience of what working people desire. It is also an amount that could be generated for life by our $1,000,000 account balance. Many clients use 7%-8% as a target for their investment returns in retirement. This is just an approximation of the average returns over time. Our Vanguard 10 provide over 10%.

Some clients transfer some of their money into a balanced fund like Wellesley Income in order to generate the income for the coming year. The balance of their tax-FREE account remains in the broad market funds we have listed above. These funds may continue to produce returns in the 10-12% range. If there is a bad year like 2008, we are not taking money out of our principal at a bad time. We take the money from a fund with 60% income-earning bonds.

The funds we have listed above include some of the most consistent low volatility returns over time. The Wellesley Income fund has produced over 10% per year on average since 1970. It contains stocks and bonds. **This fund alone might be our source** of annual withdrawals of interest and dividends. Since our **Wealth Reserve**™ is not taxable, there are no tax considerations in the decision of which fund to tap for our monthly income.

Because we have no tax liability on this income of $6,666.66 per month, we may not have to pay tax on our other income like Social Security and/or our qualified retirement funds. 85% of Social Security benefits are currently subject to federal income taxes. The IRS worksheet determines the percentage based on all our other income. Typically those with little or no other taxable income currently have no tax due on their Social Security benefits. Pensions, 401k, IRAs, and annuities are taxed as earned income since we did not pay tax on the contributions (or most of them).

In most cases, we will pay little income tax on our income in retirement since the bulk of it, $80,000 ($40,000 adjusted for inflation), will be tax-FREE. This will give us 25-30% more cash to spend compared with others who have taxable income. Pensions and other taxable income may be taxed at even higher rates in the future to pay for the two wars and two tax cuts since 2001. (We have never gone to war and taken tax breaks at the same time before so this will take time to pay off.)

Our tax-FREE income will provide us with most of our needs. If we continue to follow the same 10 steps of building wealth, we will find a comfortable lifestyle throughout the 30 to 40 years of not working unless we want to.

I and many clients are assuming we will work at least part time after we take full retirement and begin collecting Social Security. If benefits are cut, we will need to work. We are encouraged to use our tax-FREE income to develop a small business since this can help us control the income that is taxed.

As I mentioned at the beginning of this book, many working millionaires are self-employed. Running a small business is a great way to control the taxes we pay. Taxes are the biggest killer of wealth building that exists. It destroys the compounding factor.

The accumulation of $1,000,000 over time can be achieved with patience and perseverance. Spending the income that $1,000,000 can generate may require us to take some principal from time to time. If we use the same 10 steps of wealth building to do this, we will probably have enough to take care of long-term health care and other unforeseen expenses. Since we don't know what may happen, we will want to continue the same habits we have developed before retirement. We live within our means.

We may find that we will have a sizable legacy as we age. There are many ways to pass on our wealth that don't require an attorney fees and complicated legal formulations. Many clients have found that incremental gifts to charity and family provide immediate gratification. They have used the suggestions for wealth transfer Dan Keppel presented in the *Retirement Spending Plan*. amazon.com/Your-Retirement-Spending-Plan-enough/dp/1461084016/

Summary: Take $80,000 tax-FREE income each year.

This retirement income is tax-FREE and has the purchasing power of about $40,000 in today's dollars. Wealthy people who actually earned it don't go out and buy a mansion and the trappings of the wealthy when they retire. They usually have paid off their homes. They travel and share with family. Some continue to earn income doing what they enjoy or provide help to others in their volunteer efforts. Our nest egg and all the earnings are TAX-FREE. We can spend it!
This is the *Lazy Person's Way to Wealth.*

How to Buy Securities For Retirement

1. Cost matters: Broker/advisor cost 1% to 3%

If you use a salesperson, fees can cost HALF A NEST EGG!
$6,000 per year @11% for 28 years = $1, 064,740
$6,000 per year @11-1% for 28 years = $885,795
$6,000 per year @11-2% for 28 years = $738,807
$6,000 per year @11-3% for 28 years = $617,570

2. Broker/advisor stock picking does not beat index funds over the long run. No money manager has been able to beat the market consistently. No one can forecast the future.

3. Time is the key to investment success. The chance of you buying AND selling, both, at the right times, is near zero.

4. A Tax-FREE investment account increases your balance 25%.

5. Putting all your money in one stock or market sector guarantees failure over time. No one investment is perfect.

6. 'Dollar cost average' buying technique lowers the cost of shares over time. When you invest a fixed amount each month, you buy more mutual fund shares when the price is low and less when high. Over time, you will own more shares at a lower average cost.

7. If you don't have 28 years, convert your 401k or IRA to a Roth IRA paying tax as you go.

This is the Lazy Person's Way to Wealth.

Conclusion

Can you do . . . NOTHING?

It is hard to be patient and let your money grow by itself. Most people don't have the experience with a business or stocks of companies they know. They don't see the market the way that Warren Buffett does. They see it as a casino where the lucky win or a black hole where speculators lose their life savings.

According to successful investors, it is a place where the patient people are rewarded. Investors in Biogen, Qualcomm, EMC, and Kansas City Southern RR would have seen increases of 6,000% to19,000% in their accounts in the last 20 years.

The impatient stock trader would have seen an increase of 2% from buying and selling. 2%!!! 2% is less than inflation! If you knew anything about genetics, cell phones, internet or rails, you might have put your money in these businesses. All these stocks tanked for a while but the lazy person who did nothing is now wealthy. Their $2000 might be worth $400,000 now.

Most us do not know which businesses that will grow that fast in the future. We have to "settle" for the average returns of 10-12% a year. Each of our $2,000 investments would be worth about $20,000 over 20 years in a diversified group of businesses like those in the 10 Vanguard funds above.

Most of us know we will never be able to pick the right companies for the future. Wall Street tempts us by claiming they know. Some of us follow their advice and pay dearly. The industry tells us that we need them to make money. We pay them $560 billions year after year but only keep 2.56% earnings. Trading stocks does NOT benefit us. pbs.org/moyers/journal/09282007/

A person paying 1-3% of their nest egg every year to an advisor can't then admit they get very little for their money. Most advisors can't beat the investment return of the market so that $3-5,000 a year in fees is really paying for Wall Street hype. Over time that fee goes up as our balance goes up and can take up to 40% of our total possible accumulations. Advisors like to buy and sell securities creating taxes and commissions that don't help us. Large pensions don't buy and sell. businessweek.com/articles/2013-01-24/

The key to reaching our goal of $1,000,000 is compounding of high returns over time. If we pay 2% to earn 10-12%, we net 8-10%. Since we know that no advisor can guarantee 10-12% and most studies show investing directly without a "professional" can yield a better result, there is no reason to give up 2%. Advisors usually charge 1-3% whether they beat the averages or not so it is better to go for the 10-12% on our own. Sales people don't give refunds if they don't beat the market!

The clear **winning strategy** is to do nothing but invest and let compounding work its miracle. Over time using a tax-FREE account without low costs, we can accumulate enough from $250 a month each at 10-12%. Using a compounding calculator http://www.moneychimp.com/calculator/compound_interest_calcul ator.htm, we find the range is 28 to 30 years. If each spouse has an account, we can be assured of enough income no matter how long each of us lives.

If we use an advisor, we may give up over $350,000 in total accumulation. Research has shown that the average brokerage investor actually earns about **2.56%** annually. 1990-2010 (QAIB) DALBARinc.com, NOT 10-12%.

The Lazy Person's Way of building wealth works because it employs a simple strategy using a unique **tax-FREE trust account** that eliminates the biggest killer of wealth: TAXES. We have seen that compounding over time is the real engine for building wealth. Most people are NOT going to be successful at this because they don't let compounding do the work. Plus they pay high fees.

We will never be taxed on this money—it is like Uncle Sam "giving" us $350,000! We avoid the 25% Fed and 5-7% tax of most states on income from our $1 million **Wealth Reserve**™.

We can be our own masters of tax-FREE income with patience. There is no need to pick individual stocks or hire expensive advisors or product pushers with hidden fees. We can do it ourselves with our simple strategy. All we need to do is follow the plan and then do … NOTHING.

1. Create $500,000 **tax-FREE** account for the two of you.
2. Use your tax-favored lifetime investment 'bank.'
3. Compound high earnings over time.
4. Set up automatic monthly contributions for no interruptions.
5. Use low-cost mutual funds only.

6. Buy large group of stocks of growing companies worldwide.
7. Spend less than you earn.
8. Buy only the services you need—no "bells and whistles."
9. Manage the account only once a year.
10. Take $80,000 tax-FREE income each year in retirement.

You must take the first step. I don't have a product to sell you so I won't be calling you. You have to call Vanguard or TIAA-CREF yourself to set up your account. It takes about an hour to set up a Roth IRA for each of you. You can do it online or by phone. You can begin with TIAA-CREF or Vanguard. Put the contributions on automatic so you don't have to decide every month whether to invest. That is usually how people fail. Life happens and there is always an emergency that requires cash. But future life happens too and you want to be spending your $6,666 a month; not praying Washington won't cut your Social Security benefits every year.

There is a clear reason why the Lazy Person becomes wealthy. It is not luck or inheritance. Millions of immigrants to this country have done it before. They lived below their means. They saved and invested in businesses they worked. They did not let temporary cash flow problems stop them from building wealth. They used the 10 steps of building wealth every day.

As many clients say,

"I never even miss the contributions because I never see them. Then all of a sudden, I see my statement" [has $25,000, $50,000, $250,000, $1,000,000.] "We are talking real money here." That is the *Miracle of Compounding.*

Can you do just … NOTHING?

Just Relax and Keep More of What You Earn

Call Vanguard 800.551.8631 or TIAA-CREF 800.842.2888 today.
https://personal.Vanguard.com/us/ElfPDFStreamPublic?
ts=1358953111700
or
https://www.TIAA-cref.org/public/pdf/mfirains.pdf

Patience Pays!

NOTES

Goals   Time-line

Retirement $1 million

_____   _____

_____   _____

_____   _____

_____   _____

_____   _____

The Author

Law Steeple has been in financial services for over 20 years. He was a managing executive of the sales units of a number of bank securities firms. He is one of the insiders who contributed to the *The Insiders Guides* set of buyers' guides edited by Dan Keppel. The guides provide specific ways to save on all financial services. ***The Insiders' Guides to Buying Discount Financial Services: Buy Direct and Save $3,000 Every Year*** is available at Amazon, Barnes and Noble, and Abebooks.
Law lives in New Jersey and Florida.

To receive our weekly Alert with wealth-building ideas, go to www.TheInsidersGuides.com

www.ingramcontent.com/pod-product-compliance
Lightning Source LLC
Chambersburg PA
CBHW051240170526
45165CB00004B/1504